SUSAN SULTAN

Confessions of a Dachshund Owner

a wiener dog lover's advice on owning the world's most stubborn dog breed

First edition

This book was professionally typeset on Reedsy.
Find out more at reedsy.com

Contents

References

Introduction

Hello, this is a book about the marvelous Dachshund, a dog breed so charming in behavior and delightful in appearance that much of its challenging behaviors are overlooked by potential owners when choosing a dog. E. B.White, of Charlotte's Web fame, thought a book on dog training for Dachshunds was a hilarious joke. Picasso's Dachshund, Lump, was notorious for peeing on his paintings in the studio. Andy Warhol carried his Dachshund, Archie, in his arms everywhere like a fashion accessory. Stories about Dachshunds abound. Mostly due to their bad behavior. Lucky for them that they are so darned cute.

This is a book based on my own experiences. Once you acquire a Dachshund you will find yourself a member of an enormous family of other Dachshund owners who adore their dogs. You will hear and relate to many of the same tales. This is a book that I have written to alert you to some of the mistakes that I made in raising and training my own two Dachshunds in order that you might not make the ones that I did. Of course, as their owner, I was totally smitten with my Dachshunds no matter how they turned out.

I got my first Dachshund, Louie, when I was going through the break up of my marriage. I wanted a puppy to give me solace from my heartache. On a trip to the Lake District in England I met a little wirehaired

Dachshund named Susie and decided on the spot that was the breed I wanted. But then one day, on a walk near my home in New York City, I passed by a small pet store. In the window were a bunch of roly-poly puppies playing. Under a pile of them lay a small black and tan Dachshund who didn't seem to mind the others on top of him. We looked at each other and I immediately fell for him. My best friend bought him for me. Two days later I picked him up and took him back to my apartment. I was completely naive. I hadn't had a dog since I was a kid. But how hard could it be?

I named him Louie and he became my little soulmate for 17 years. Later I would find a female friend for him, another black and tan Dachshund that I named Ava. She was with me for 15 years. I thought of them as my glamorous Hollywood couple, Ava and Louie, sleek and shiny with fabulous profiles.

I learned so much.

1

About Dachshunds

Dachshund Physical Traits

Before you get a Dachshund you need to know as much as you can about the breed. There are three types of Dachshunds all based on their coat type: long-haired, short haired and wire-haired. There are two sizes: miniature and standard. There are many markings and color variations from a unicolor of red, brown and yellow to two colors like black and tan to the many patterned brindle and piebald. They all have the similar body types of long low bodies with short legs and long ears. Their chests seem large relative to the rest of their bodies. Their heads have a tapered nose. This combination of features leads to a very singular looking dog which I could never quite believe exists. There are no other dogs like Dachshunds.

I chose my black and tan miniature Dachshund because I liked the clean sleek look of their coats. Louie and Ava sometimes reminded me of otters and seals. They always had dark shiny coats even in old age. I was happy with them being miniatures because I thought they would be easy to pick up and carry if I needed to get them away from other dogs or children. I liked to travel a lot and I could transport them easily on planes and trains. Then Louie actually grew bigger than a miniature. He was around 20 pounds. I was still able to pick him up which I was really thankful for many times. Always take care of delicate backs when picking up your dog.

Dachshund Mental Traits

The most important behavior trait to remember is that Dachshunds were bred over a long span of time to be hunters, specifically to go down in tunnels after vicious badgers. Many of their actions stem from this one fact. They were bred to be very independently minded and to think quickly on their own yet they are strongly loyal to a master. Besides having the hunting instinct they are very curious, playful and loving. They will entertain you for hours with their funny antics. Dachshunds love being around humans and expect to get a lot of attention and petting.

2

Dachshund Puppies

Once you have decided to get a Dachshund you have several choices of where to acquire your dog. I have read that many of the pet shop puppies come from puppy mills. I believe Louie probably came from one. His papers showed that he was born in Oklahoma. His father's name was Freeway. I pictured his dad on a motorcycle wearing a black leather jacket. I don't think you can really tell what you are getting from a pet shop. Check out its reputation. Make sure the puppies look well cared for and clean. I was lucky.

Breeders may offer more reliable information especially if you are able to visit the puppies, see how they are being treated and meet their parents. Ava came from a breeder but I didn't know, at the time, what kind of questions to ask. Ava was already two years old when I got her. The breeders had a small army of Dachshunds in their backyard. They were moving out of state and selling off their puppies. The puppies looked healthy, happy and clean. Ava was small and had those beguiling Dachshund eyes that melt your heart in an instant.

With rescued dogs try and get as much information about the dog as you can. Know that you may have things come up that take more time and energy than you expected to deal with. But it may be well worth it to make an abandoned dog a new loving home.

No matter where you get your Dachshund, be sure and collect all the information and records of health vaccinations of your puppy and keep them in a safe place.

Making Your Home Ready

It is an exciting moment when you first bring your puppy home and show its new surroundings to it. The most important thing to remember is that it takes time for a puppy to get used to the new environment. It's best to keep any chaos to a minimum.

The new puppy will need:

- Puppy food
- Food and water bowl- aluminum is recommended - less possibility of bacteria
- Collar and ID
- Leash and harness (needed to keep Dachshund backs healthy)
- Poop bags
- Pee pads
- Toys and Treats
- Dog bed
- Crate and blanket
- Flea and tick medication
- Brush

- Nail clippers
- Ramps and stairs to protect from stress on backs
- Bringing Home the Puppy

It's a big day when you first bring home the puppy. It's helpful to bring a friend along to lend a helping hand. A helpful tip is to also bring home some of the bedding that the puppy has been using to give the newcomer some comfort. Limit excitement in the surroundings during its first days while acclimating itself to new surroundings.

When I got Ava, my second Dachshund, I had moved from New York City to the Berkshires in western Massachusetts to an old two story house on a charming street lined with trees. It had a slightly formal fenced-in garden in the front. The street had nice sidewalks, neighbors were friendly and lots of people walked by with their dogs on the way to town.

I took a friend with me and drove to NJ to check out Ava who I had scoped out on line. Louie was about four at the time. He came with us. I picked up the new pup, held her in my lap wrapped in her bedding on the drive home. She looked up at me the whole way back with those big Dachshund eyes. You'll get to know the Dachshund gaze once you get one. They are heartbreaking. Louie rode in the back seat eager to meet his new companion.

When we got home my son was there with a friend. He was touring with a band and they had a stopover nearby so he came to see me. I put Ava and her bedding in a quiet room and left the guys to go to the grocery store to buy food so we could make dinner.

When I got back the guys were frantic. They had let Ava out by mistake and she had taken off through the unfamiliar neighborhood at high speed. They chased her down the streets and through backyards but couldn't catch her. They were both exhausted and freaked out. I headed out looking for her but never even spotted her. That night I went to bed heartbroken. I lost her the very first day I got her. Before I went to bed I put her bedding out on the front porch hoping she might catch a scent of it. Around 2:00AM I heard a dog barking. I ran downstairs and there she was on the porch with her bedding. It was a miracle. I couldn't believe it. The power of the Dachshund nose!

The Veterinarians

The new puppy will need to be checked out by a reputable veterinarian and given the preliminary shots it may not have gotten yet. Shots and check ups need to be kept up on a regular basis. The vet can also recommend food suitable for a puppy.

Dachshund puppies are extra active. My vet suggested leaving Louie with him for a few hours as he had an emergency when we arrived at the office. When I came back, he said he could not believe how active Louie was, jumping up and down on chairs, snooping in every corner and running around the office like a maniac. Then he said he remembered he was a Dachshund and it made perfect sense. Keep this in mind as you acclimate them in your home.

Chewing

If you don't want your shoes destroyed by a little puppy, put them and any other chewable item away, far away. I always kept a supply of chewy toys for little teeth handy in a basket on the floor. The key to keeping them from chewing your things is to make sure they have their things to keep them occupied. Louie especially loved to pull the stuffing out of every dog bed I ever bought him and within the first ten minutes that I gave it to him. I spent a lot of time restuffing and sewing up the beds just to have them torn up time after time. I even put his chewy toys in his bed but he would still dump them out and go for the stuffing. I never solved that one but at least he never bothered my shoes or furniture legs.

Indoors and outdoors

I lived in New York City when Louie was a pup. The veterinarian advised me not to take him out on the street until he was 16 weeks old. That was to protect him from being exposed to diseases like distemper and viruses until his vaccinations were complete. Most vets recommend this or even longer.

Of course, you will need to take your dog outside to relieve itself. I carried Louie to the small park across the street to pee until he could walk on a leash.

Another reason for keeping your dog inside is that the puppy might eat something on the street or yard that is bad for it. Strangely, the streets of New York seemed to always have a lot of chicken bones in the gutters. I never saw people eating chicken on the street. Why were there always bones? I had to be very diligent to keep Louie from finding them and other disgusting things that probably smelled really good to him.

Doggy Day Care

Doggy daycare can also begin at 16 weeks. This is great for socializing your pet with other dogs, lessen any separation anxiety and burn off extra energy. Many doggy day cares offer obedience training for an extra fee as well.

When Louie was almost grown he was in a doggie day care close by my apartment. He loved going. His best friend was a black and white great dane named Daisy. They were inseparable and I loved watching them play together.

One day I picked him up and walked him home. He seemed a little off. I didn't think that much about it but in the apartment he seemed dazed. "Louie, Louie," I kept repeating. He wouldn't even look at me. He peered off into the distance. I was beginning to worry. Suddenly I realized it wasn't Louie. It was another black and tan dachshund that looked just like him. I raced the worried guy back to doggie daycare hoping I would get there before the other owners took Louie to their home. And there he was in the playroom sitting by Daisy waiting to go home. I often wonder what that other little Dachshund was thinking as I walked him to my apartment. "Who the heck is this person and where are they taking me?"

Puppy Training

Most guidebooks will tell you that before you get a dog you should have some idea of how you are going to train it. All dogs are pack animals. There is a hierarchy within the pack with the Alpha dog as the leader. You, the owner, should pattern yourself as the Alpha dog. This makes perfect sense intellectually but up against a willful Dachshund it takes time and persistence to implement. If you are not a domineering type or follow certain steps, the Dachshund will take the role of the Alpha dog.

Some training methods are stricter than others. I personally found the plans that outlined the privileges of the Alpha dog too harsh and more than I could follow. Many suggested that the owner's bed should be off limits as it is the special right of the Alpha. Several rooms of your choice could be off limits determined again by the Alpha. Others dictated the dog should not be fed until after the owner has eaten. Some also restricted petting time that was rigorously controlled by the owner.

I, and I am sorry to say, did not adhere to these rules. In my mind there is no feeling greater than having dogs sleeping in the bed with you. Their little warm bellies are like hot water bottles. Their little snoring sounds are like lullabies. Dachshunds like to burrow under the covers. I found this adorable. You will get used to finding them under any pile of clothes on the floor or under your blankets at the bottom of the bed. Many times you may wonder how they can still breathe under the weight. One has to be cautious of where you sit with a Dachshund in the house. Very likely you'll end up sitting on the animal more than once.

Looking back, I wish I had made more of an effort to be the Alpha in my pack. I would have granted them most of their desires but would have had the option not to if it seemed best. As it turned out, they basically ruled.

So do you even want the dog up on the furniture? In your bed? At the door when guests arrive? Think about these issues before you bring home the puppy. Once they start these behaviors it is hard to change. By maintaining dominance over the animal it will naturally look to you for guidance. It's a good idea to know beforehand what you expect of them and they of you.

One area of training I wish that I had adhered to was advice on housebreaking. It would have made my life easier in the long run. The other was teaching basic commands. I urge you to set aside a large amount of time and patience for these two issues which are discussed further in the book.

Housebreaking the Puppy

Dachshunds are notoriously hard to housebreak. Puppies need to relieve themselves about every two hours. In the city and country, even at less than 16 weeks, they need to be taken out to a grassy or convenient spot to go to the bathroom. They will go back to that spot repeatedly. You have to make time in your training to do this.

You can also paper train them on puppy pads. But puppies and grown dogs don't always make it just on the pee pads. And as they grow older there is a lot more pee. Once they have been trained on the pads it can be difficult to get them to go outdoors.

For me, when I lived in a city apartment, there was the question of taking them out in the middle of the night. At two in the morning in New York City I didn't want to get dressed, take an elevator down eight flights and go out onto a dark city street. So I took the route of having the pee pads at night and taking them out during the day. When I moved to where I had a yard I tried to get rid of the pads but it was too late. They never adjusted. They never learned to go to the door and scratch or whine to go out. They just didn't seem to mind peeing in the house on the pads or maybe not on the pads. I was not alone with this problem. So many Dachshund owners have told me that they could never fully train theirs as well.

One other problem with housebreaking Dachshunds is that they abhor going out in the rain or snow. They will just flat out refuse. It's another good reason to be able to pick them up and place them in the yard though most likely they will run straight back to the door to get in.

The issue of housebreaking is a big one with this breed. Other dog owners will think you are totally at fault in your training. And it adds to the odor of the house which you will end up endlessly cleaning. Double down on the training in the beginning and maybe, just maybe, you will avoid this. Good luck.

Puppy Training

Most puppy training starts with the command "sit." The basic training method is positive reinforcement and repetition. Place the puppy at your feet, hold a treat over his head. He will try to grab it. When he gets tired and sits then give him the treat as you say the command "sit". Repeat this. Practice training in short sessions. It will take repeating many times. Just be patient.

One of the most important training commands is getting the puppy to come when called. Most training manuals suggest not using their name to call them just the word "come" or "here". Start with training treats and your puppy not too far away at a time that he is probably hungry. Use the command in an excited friendly voice. It will most likely come to you and then you reward it with a treat. Repeating this should bring success. Then take the training further by moving further and further away from the dog before you call.

My dogs, both of them, never ever could be trained to come. Louie and I went to obedience school. We both failed. I ended up crying every session. He might do something for a moment, would get bored and refuse to move. It was painful. I gave up. The teachers were even exasperated. Dachshunds can be really tough.

Ava was two when I got her. I tried to train her to come. It was hopeless. My sister, who always had eager trainable dogs, thought there was something wrong with her brain. I think it was just a Dachshund mindset. Her previous owners were a handsome Russian couple. One day I thought she might come to Russian commands. I was excited to try. I looked up "come" in Russian. I took her outside, put her down and had a treat in my pocket. I moved a few feets away and said, "Ko mne." She came right away. I was overjoyed. I gave her a treat. I'd broken the code I thought. We tried again. Nothing. And she never ever came when I called again.

Walking the Puppy

Training a puppy to walk on a leash should be done with acquainting it with wearing the harness in the house for short periods of time. Then gradually attach the leash and let it walk around with it while still in the house. Walking the dog outside should also be done in short periods building up to longer ones. Try to walk the dog with the leash being loose. Take treats with you. When another dog approaches or something else distracts it use the treats to grab its attention. This goes for barking too. Try and distract from barking before it happens with a treat. Soon you will be using the treats less and less as time goes by. If the puppy pulls and tries to go another way, remain totally still until the puppy comes back to you. With Dachshunds this could take awhile. Remain calm. I found that by picking them up and carrying them a short distance the way you want to go would usually break the stand off. I don't know if trainers would approve of my solution. It worked for me.

Walks are a great time to let the puppy enjoy sniffing and exploring the world of smells. Keep a close watch for any thing they may pick up. They can grab and swallow unwanted things quickly.

Walking a Dachshund can also be challenging. Louie, as a puppy, on our walks attracted a lot of attention. Shop keepers would come out and give him treats. As he grew older they would wave us in as we passed. Everyone wanted to pet him and give him a snack. He had a certain path on our walks that would take us by his favorite shops. The walk would end near the door of our apartment building where a street food vendor would flick a bit of chicken for him on the sidewalk. He had a large fan club and we couldn't escape it by walking in another direction.

People love a wiener dog.

Socializing

Dachshunds are a friendly breed. It's important to start a puppy early on being around people, children and other dogs when they are old enough. Keep a sharp eye out on their behavior and monitor children to make sure they are gentle with the dog. Failure to socialize the dog can make them lonely and may cause them to develop anxiety and fear of separation.

Nipping and Barking

Keeping your Dachshund occupied and exercised helps reduce their need to bark. In my home in the Berkshires Louie was a barker. Ava would follow his lead and bark, too. Louie would perch on the back of the sofa and peer out into the street. I think he felt a responsibility to keep an eye on the activities in the neighborhood. When we moved away from that house to where there weren't many passing by he calmed down. My nearby neighbors never complained but were probably glad to see us go. In New York he would bark at sounds in the apartment building's hallway but never prolonged sessions of barking. He had a pretty full schedule of dog parks, long walks and doggie daycare. Some dogs bark continuously out of loneliness or anxiety and it may be helpful to call a trainer in to help remedy the situation.

Digging

Most Dachshunds love to dig. Their large front paws and strong front legs were built for that. They have an acutely sensitive sense of smell. Dachshunds can actually breathe in and out at the same time. That is how they manage to stay down in tunnels for a long time. My Dachshunds sometimes got obsessed if they caught a sniff of something they wanted. They would just start manically digging. Luckily that rarely happened but I do still find holes they dug. Better to fill them up. It is easy to twist an ankle if you accidentally step in one. In the city Louie was intensely attracted to the smells coming up from the subway entrances. He would stand at the top of the stairs and refuse to move. It was one of his great desires – to go down into the underground. That, and to catch a squirrel.

3

The Adult Dachshund

By the time Louie was fully grown we had moved to a small town in the Berkshires. I added Ava to the mix. It is amazing how many people, after getting one Dachshund, add another. It just seems natural. And it combats the dog getting lonely which can lead to excessive barking and aggression. At our new house we had a fenced in yard and went on walks every day in the neighborhood and on trails. We spent a lot of time in the dog park.

Louie had grown into a typical Dachshund who considered himself to be the Alpha dog around other dogs. Yes, he did have a big personality. He held himself elegantly, his behavior was imperious and I generally called him King Louie. I was just one of his loyal subjects.

Dachshunds are very prone to the Napoleon Canine Syndrome along with other small dogs. Some bad behaviors this can inspire are aggression, growling, not obeying commands and begging for food among others.

At the dog park Louie played with the big boys. He wasn't interested in the small dog area. Periodically he would hop up on the bench where I was sitting and peer down on the other dogs before joining them again for some rough play. Ava on the other hand, was rather delicate and shy. She walked with a very fetching swivel of her hips and didn't generally like being with bigger dogs. She would walk around the edge of the park and then come over to me and sit at my feet watching the others.

Together they could egg each other on when they felt safe enough to misbehave or something or someone in their environment needed straightening out. I only saw Louie run once out of fear from a crazed little Dachshund up the street. She chased him all the way home and he scratched frantically at the door to get it.

Many Dachshunds bond deeply with their owners. Louie and Ava were very loyal and protective of me though not very obedient. Unfortunately we got into trouble. Walking two dogs can be hard to handle if the dogs get distracted by something or an event. They were usually good about running into other dogs. Friendly for a moment and then on their way. What they didn't like were surprises. One day a sudden appearance of a jogger's sneakered feet pounding by them on the payment startled and upset them. They both went, unexpectedly, for the jogger's heels. I don't know which one it was that bit her but the jogger's skin was broken. The jogger was understandably irate. She said it kept happening to her. I thought maybe she shouldn't run right through the middle of a bunch of dogs again. I apologized profusely. I may have even sent flowers, I can't remember. Anyway, she informed the town's animal control. I produced their up to date immunization records but they quarantined them for a month or more. I was very distressed. At least the jogger didn't sue me like the mailman who sued my friends after their dog bit him. But now they had a record. I decided then and there to find another house outside of town where they could have a bigger fenced area and be away from the constant flow of people and traffic. Luckily I found a perfect spot a mile from town with a pastoral view and a big backyard. Louie missed monitoring the neighborhood but found new interest in squirrels and rabbits.

Travel

Dachshunds are perfect dogs to go on trips with you depending on their personality. Their compact size and shape make them easily fit into a carrier. If they have been socialized fairly well they won't tend to bark or be aggressive. I made several plane trips with Louie under my seat in a carrier. He was a perfect little traveler.

Both of my Dachshunds also rode in trains and behaved well. They were not in carriers but on leashes.

One particular trip from Grand Central Station to upstate New York was memorable. I had left my car in the station and had come into the city with Louie. I still had my apartment there. It was the middle of winter and a big snowstorm hit while I was there. After it stopped I planned to head back up to the station where I left my car and go back to our home in the Berkshires. I hadn't prepared myself for the storm and had no shovel in the car in case I had to dig my way out of the snow so I went into a hardware store in the city to get one. All they had was a big orange oversized plastic one. I bought it.

I arrived in Grand Central station with the shovel over my shoulder, carrying my overnight bag and Louie on a leash. The station was crowded with travelers hurriedly criss-crossing the Grand Concourse.

Halfway to the train Louie suddenly wiggled off his leash and ran off into the crowd. I think I screamed and tried to make my way after him. Amazingly, the crowd sort of parted for us as I chased him and several other people joined in the chase. Someone finally caught him, I put him back on the leach, the crowd engulfed us once more. We just made the train - me with the shovel, the bag and the dog. It was a good thing too because we arrived at my car before it got dark. Indeed I had to shovel out the wheels in the cold to get out. I think we both slept well that night, happy to be safe in the bed.

Feeding the Adult Dog

It seems like most dogs live to eat, not eat to live. Your dog's veterinarian will be able to recommend the food best suited to your dog and its health. As it ages and issues come up, there are certain diets that will help the dog live its best and longest life. I tested out several different types of dog food, from wet to dry, from raw to canned. I found my dogs liked a little variety and changed around the brands as they got bored with one. I tried to find and buy the healthiest brands from reviews and articles. Check for ones with high quality protein.

It is fairly easy to overfeed your Dachshunds. They are prone to gaining weight so it is important to help them maintain a healthy weight. One reason for that especially is that it is bad for their long backs to carry too much weight. Too many treats can also add to the additional weight. Also feeding them human food from the table not only is bad for them it encourages the nasty habit of begging. Once you start it is almost impossible to get them to stop. Adequate exercise is a must for all dogs no matter what breed.

Below is a list of foods and other things that dogs should not eat and can be toxic to your pet.

- Chocolate
- Raisins and grapes
- Avocado
- Food sweetened with xylitol
- Alcohol
- Coffee and tea
- Cinnamon
- Onions
- Garlic
- Chives
- Macadamia nuts
- Ice cream
- Apple, cherry, apricot and plum seeds
- Mushrooms
- Nutmeg
- Uncooked dough and yeast
- Fatty cuts of meat
- Bones
- Dairy
- Bacon
- Corn on cob
- White bread
- Salty snacks

Here is a list of things they can safely eat.

- Carrots
- Cucumbers
- Celery
- Rice
- Cooked pumpkin
- Salmon
- Cooked eggs
- Cooked corn
- Unsalted cashews and peanuts
- Blueberries
- Oranges apples bananas
- Watermelon, peaches
- Green peas
- Chicken and turkey
- Shrimp and fish
- Oats and wheat

Make sure your dog's water bowl is always filled. It is easy to overlook so remember to keep an eye on it. And you don't want your dog to drink out of puddles and other water sources while on your walks. They may be contaminated with parasites, bacteria or viruses

Teeth

Dachshunds are prone to having teeth issues. To get the best results and prevent gum disease they should have their teeth cleaned by a professional at the veterinarians. Depending upon the dog's age and health, this will entail putting them under an anesthetic. Their health care professionals will take every precaution to ensure their safety. Also, be aware that canine dental care can become costly so plan ahead.

It is also recommended to brush the dog's teeth every day with especially formulated toothpaste for dogs. This was something that I did not do religiously and wish that I had. It's not an easy job but the dogs do get used to it and it does prevent loss of teeth.

Flea and Tick Prevention

The veterinarians will advise you on the best methods of prevention. Most offices sell approved treatments without harmful ingredients. Keep tick removers on hand and check for ticks after outings even in your own backyard. Ticks can carry harmful diseases such as Lyme disease.

My dog, Ava, was having trouble walking with her back legs. After rushing her to the vets they tested her for Lyme which it turned out she had. She was put on antibiotics and recovered. I hadn't been aware that was one of the symptoms of the disease. Make sure you keep up with your dog's Lyme vaccination.

Heartworm

Heartworm is one of the most deadly threats to your dog's health. You should consistently give your dog medication against this condition. Heartworm disease treatment is expensive and lengthy and the disease can permanently damage the dog's heart.

Eye Care

Dachshunds are prone to getting cataracts. My dog, Louie, developed them during his old age. It did not seem to cause him any anxiety or slow him down. He knew his own territory and seemed content to live within it. He lived to the ripe old age of 17.

Back Problems

Back problems are a very big issue for Dachshunds. The length of their spine makes it very easy for them to injure it. Also, due to their energetic lifestyle, (jumping on furniture and beds, racing up and down stairs, chasing other dogs in the dog park, etc.) they can weaken the spine and eventually cause an injury. It is imperative that if you notice them having trouble walking that you take the dog to the vet's *immediately*. Otherwise they can end up with permanent damage.

Here is Louie's back story. After our move out of New York we lived in a house with very steep stairs. Louie would shoot up and down them like a mad man. One day I noticed he was having trouble walking. I was concerned and called the vet for an appointment the next day. As the day went on he was having more and more trouble. By nightfall he was not moving and was trembling, a sign of pain. I was up all night with him, worried to death. The next morning we went to the vets. She took one look at him and said I had to take him to Cummings School of Veterinary Medicine at Tufts University not far from Boston right away. They would probably have to perform an operation on his spine. If I wasted another minute he might be permanently paralyzed. She said it was a wonderful hospital. She knew the doctors there and would call ahead.

It was the middle of the winter. I got in the car and took off down the turnpike towards the hospital. On arriving they checked him in right away. They returned to me in a few minutes. Yes, he had injured his spine and he needed an operation. I would have to leave him there for several days. I signed the papers and left. It was night by now, a snow storm enveloped me on the turnpike and I cried the whole way home.

The operation went well though they didn't know if he would ever walk again. If not he would have to be in a little chariot for his back legs to be mobile. I brought him home and started nursing him back to health. I was so glad to see him. I made a nest for him on one of the couches in the living room. He had a long cut down the length of his spine. Then I got to learn the art of expressing the pee of a dog. I never in a million years thought I could do that. But I did learn to do it and even got used to doing it. Slowly over several months he got better. He started showing some signs of movement in his legs. Eventually he regained full use of his back legs and you would never know he was injured except for a faint scar down his back. The moral of the story is protect your Dachshund's back at all costs. The Tufts hospital told me they do an incredible amount of these operations each day. Louie was one of the lucky ones. He regained his ability to walk. Others do not. Though they can adapt to the little chariots, I have seen it shorten the length of their lives. Pick up your Dachshunds holding them carefully under the body supporting their spines. Install ramps to go upstairs and outdoors. Use doggie stairs to get on and off the beds. Discourage them from leaping and jumping when out on a walk. Know your closest trauma veterinary office and how to get there just in case.

With that dramatic story I will end this short book of my advice for Dachshund owners. A lot of this is based on my personal experience and the mistakes that I made in raising my pets. They both had exceptionally long and mostly healthy lives even though I wasn't as diligent and smart about training as I should have been. I admit I probably wasn't the optimal personality type to raise the best behaved wiener dog. But I loved them with all my heart. I was completely mesmerized by them. They entertained me by the hour, comforted me like little Mother Teresas in my ups and downs.

When Ava got sick and died, her organs failing, I didn't know how I would survive. Then less than two weeks later Louie died, I think of a broken heart. I hung their collars on a nail above my bed so that I would have sweet dreams of them. Now I am totally addicted to watching the hundreds of video snippets of Dachshunds on the internet. My devotion to the breed is unlimited. I hope, if you adopt a Dachshund that you, too, will have the time of your lives together.

References

Dale C. Randall, Dachshund Survival Guide, 2024. (n.d.).

Kaiser, C. (2020a). *Dachshund Training Vol 2: Dog Training for your grown-up Dachshund.* Expertengruppe Verlag.

Kaiser, C. (2020b). *Dachshund training: Dog Training for your Dachshund puppy.* Expertengruppe Verlag.

Kaiser, C. (2021). *Dachshund Training Vol 3 - Taking care of your*

Dachshund: Nutrition, Common Diseases and General Care of Your Dachshund. Expertengruppe Verlag.

Oakhurst Veterinary Hospital - Dental care. (n.d.). oakhurstvet.com. https://www.oakhurstvet.com/services/dental-care.html

Richie, V. (2020). *The complete guide to Dachshunds: Finding, Feeding, Training, Caring For, Socializing, and Loving Your New Dachshund Puppy.* LP Media Inc.

Streisand, E. D., & Picard, C. (March 14, 2018). !6 Foods Your Dog Should Never Eat. *Good Housekeeping.*

Made in the USA
Monee, IL
14 November 2024

70146555R00021